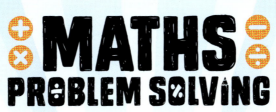

MATHS
PROBLEM SOLVING

NATURE

by Anita Loughrey

CONTENTS

INTRODUCTION

Context-based maths gives you a purpose for using maths, and cements your understanding of both why and how maths is applied to daily life. This book explores a range of numeracy skills and topics through 13 different real-life scenarios.

At the head of each section, there's a quick visual guide to the topic and skills covered. The introduction to each section sets the scene and presents the maths question that will be answered.

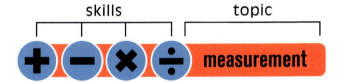

Then you are guided through the process of answering the question, step by step.

In addition, each section also contains helpful tips and an extra challenge: **Now try this** ...

There's an answer key for the **Now try this** ... challenge at the end of the book and words covered in the glossary are highlighted in **bold** throughout the text.

HOW MANY WINGS CAN YOU SEE?

You count 8 dragonflies and 7 crane flies flying around the pond in the park. How many wings you can see altogether?

Dragonflies have 4 wings. It will be quicker and easier to use the 4 times table than to count up in groups of 4, 8 times.

4, 8, 12, 16, 20, 24, 28, 32, 36, 40, 44, 48

There are 8 dragonflies, with 4 wings each.

8 x 4 = 32

So, 8 dragonflies have 32 wings altogether.

Now you need to calculate how many crane fly wings there are. Each one has 2 wings and there are 7 of them.

2 x 7 = 14

So, 7 crane flies have 14 wings altogether.

Add up your totals: 32 + 14 = 46

 You can see a total of 46 insect wings fluttering over the pond!

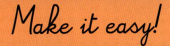

Memorise your **times tables** up to and including the 12 times table to make calculations quicker and easier.

Add or multiply to answer questions ending with 'altogether' or 'in total' Subtract to answer questions ending with 'are left?'

Now try this...

If each dragonfly damages 1 wing, how many working dragonfly wings are left?

HOW TALL ARE THE SHORTEST SUNFLOWERS?

You and your brother are growing sunflowers. Your brother's tallest sunflower is 36 centimetres tall. Your shortest sunflower is double this height. How tall is it? Your brother's shortest sunflower is half the size of his tallest one. How tall is it?

To work out double 36 you can add 36 and 36 or multiply 36 by 2.

36 + 36 = 72
36 x 2 = 72

Your shortest sunflower is 72 centimetres tall.

To work out the height of your brother's shortest sunflower you have to halve 36 or divide 36 by 2.

36 ÷ 2 = 18

Your brother's shortest sunflower is 18 centimetres tall.

To **double** a number, you **multiply** it by **2**.

Double 18 = 18 x 2 = 36

Double 12 = 12 x 2 = 24

Double 9 = 9 x 2 = 18

Double 6 = 6 x 2 = 12

Halving is the opposite of doubling.

To **half** a number you **divide** it by **2**.

Half of 36 = 36 ÷ 2 = 18

Half of 24 = 24 ÷ 2 = 12

Half of 18 = 18 ÷ 2 = 9

Half of 12 = 12 ÷ 2 = 6

Now try this...

Your tallest sunflower is double the height of your shortest sunflower.

How tall does your sunflower grow?

Your shortest sunflower is 72 centimetres tall. Your brother's shortest sunflower is 18 centimetres tall.

WHAT FRACTION OF THE RABBITS ARE EATING?

You go for a walk in the country and see a field with 12 rabbits in it. Your sister tells you that 2/6 of the rabbits are playing in the sun and the rest are eating. Can you work out the fraction of rabbits that are eating?

1											
1/3				1/3				1/3			
1/6		1/6		1/6		1/6		1/6		1/6	
1/12	1/12	1/12	1/12	1/12	1/12	1/12	1/12	1/12	1/12	1/12	1/12

If you count the number of thirds in the table, you can see there are 3. $\frac{3}{3}$ is the same as 1.

$\frac{1}{3} + \frac{1}{3} + \frac{1}{3} = \frac{3}{3} = 1$

There are $\frac{6}{6}$ in the table, and they are equal to 1, too.

$\frac{1}{6} + \frac{1}{6} + \frac{1}{6} + \frac{1}{6} + \frac{1}{6} + \frac{1}{6} = \frac{6}{6} = 1$

12 twelfths are the same as 1, too.

To make a whole number, the **numerator** (the top number) and the **denominator** (the bottom number) need to be the same.

So, if $\frac{2}{6}$ of the total $\frac{6}{6}$ rabbits are playing, you need to do the sum:

$\frac{6}{6} - \frac{2}{6} = \frac{4}{6}$

So, $\frac{4}{6}$ of the rabbits are not playing. They are eating.

1					
$\frac{1}{3}$		$\frac{1}{3}$		$\frac{1}{3}$	
$\frac{1}{6}$	$\frac{1}{6}$	$\frac{1}{6}$	$\frac{1}{6}$	$\frac{1}{6}$	$\frac{1}{6}$
$\frac{1}{12}$ $\frac{1}{12}$	$\frac{1}{12}$ $\frac{1}{12}$	$\frac{1}{12}$ $\frac{1}{12}$	$\frac{1}{12}$ $\frac{1}{12}$	$\frac{1}{12}$ $\frac{1}{12}$	$\frac{1}{12}$ $\frac{1}{12}$

Look at the yellow section. $\frac{1}{3}$ is the same as $\frac{2}{6}$ and $\frac{4}{12}$. Because they are the same size, these fractions are called **equivalent** fractions.

Look at the orange section. $\frac{1}{6}$ is the same as $\frac{2}{12}$. These fractions are equivalent fractions, too.

The best fractions to give as answers are fractions that use the smallest numbers. You make a fraction smaller, or simplify it, by dividing the numerator and the denominator by the same number.

You know $\frac{4}{6}$ of the rabbits are eating. 4 and 6 can both be divided by 2:

$4 \div 2 = 2$
$6 \div 2 = 3$

So the simplified fraction is $\frac{2}{3}$.

You can tell your sister that $\frac{2}{3}$ of the rabbits are eating.

A **mnemonic** to help you remember: The **numerator** needs to nod above the line. The **denominator** dances down below.

Divide or **multiply** the **denominator** and the **numerator** by the same number to find **equivalent fractions.**

$\frac{1}{2} = \frac{2}{4} = \frac{3}{6} = \frac{4}{8} = \frac{5}{10} = \frac{6}{12}$

$\frac{1}{3} = \frac{2}{6} = \frac{3}{9} = \frac{4}{12} = \frac{5}{15} = \frac{6}{18}$

$\frac{1}{4} = \frac{2}{8} = \frac{3}{12} = \frac{4}{16} = \frac{5}{20} = \frac{6}{24}$

Now try this...

$\frac{6}{12}$ of the rabbits go into their warren for a nap. What fraction of the rabbits are still outside? What is the smallest **equivalent fraction**?

WHAT'S THE PERIMETER OF THE WILDLIFE GARDEN?

Your school is going to build a fence all the way around its new wildlife garden. Two of the measurements are missing. Can you work out the **perimeter** to find out how long the fence needs to be?

28 m

16 m

14 m

The perimeter is the total length of all the sides of a two-dimensional (2D) shape. To find the perimeter, you must add up the lengths of each of the sides.

This drawing is not to scale so you can't measure the missing sides to find the perimeter. You need to look at the information provided. You know the lengths of 4 of the sides. By subtracting the shorter length from the longer length opposite it, you can work out the lengths of the missing measurements.

28 – 14 = 14 metres
16 – 8 = 8 metres

8 m

Now add the lengths of all the sides together to find out the perimeter.

Take a look at the drawing again to spot the quickest way to do this. 14 and 14 is equal to 28, and 8 and 8 is equal to 16.

14 x 2 = 28
8 x 2 = 16

To work out the perimeter you can add these totals together and then multiply them by 2.

28 + 16 = 44
44 x 2 = 88 metres

The perimeter of the wildlife garden is 88 metres so you will need 88 metres of fence.

Make it easy!

Keep sums simple by removing **units of measurement** before you start. But remember to put them back when you write your **final answer.**

Make sure you **count all the sides!** Put a dot in one corner and write down each length until you get back to the dot.

Now try this...

The school decides to make the **length** of the wildlife garden **5 metres longer.**

What is the **perimeter** of the wildlife garden now?

WHAT KIND OF ANGLE IS IT?

You are picking apples from the tree in your garden. There are lots of different **angles** in its branches. Can you name the angles?

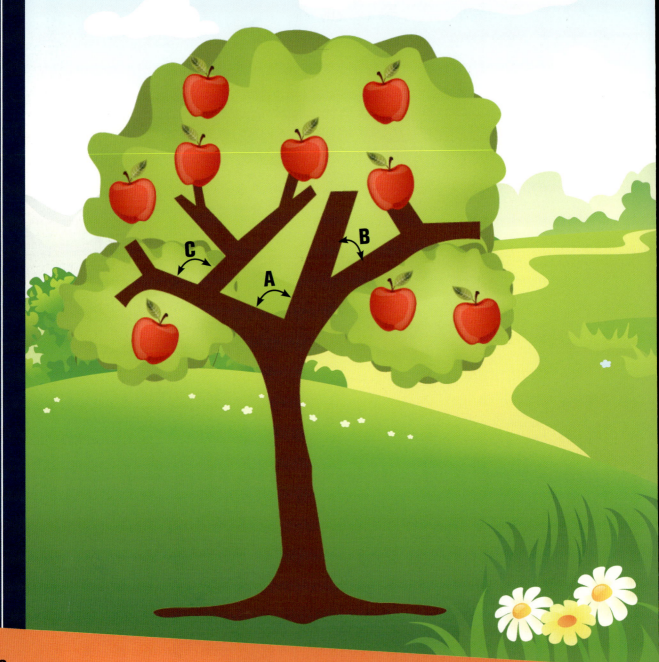

Angles have different names according to their size. A right angle is exactly 90 degrees. An angle less than 90 degrees is called an acute angle. An angle greater than a right angle is called an obtuse angle.

Angle A looks like it might be a right angle. Check this by folding a piece of paper exactly in half and then half again. Place the square corner you have made over A. If the square corner fits A exactly, it is a right angle.

Now check if B and C are greater or less than a right angle, using the square corner you have made.

B is less than a right angle. You can write this as: B < a right angle.

An angle less than a right angle is called an acute angle. So B is an acute angle.

C is greater than a right angle. You can write this as: C > a right angle.

An angle greater than a right angle is an obtuse angle. So C is an obtuse angle.

Let's put this information in a table:

Angle	Guess	Measure	Type of angle
A	A right angle	90°	Right
B	< right angle	< 90°	Acute
C	> right angle	> 90°	Obtuse

 Now you know A is a right angle, B is an acute angle and C is an obtuse angle.

Make it easy!

> greater than
< less than
= equal to

Mnemonic to help you remember:

Obtuse angles are wide and thick!

Acute angles can snap shut quick!

Now try this...

How many **obtuse angles** can you see in the tree altogether?

HOW MANY MORE LADYBIRDS ARE THERE THAN SPIDERS?

Your class spent 20 minutes counting minibeasts in the wildlife garden and then you put all the **data** in a **bar chart**. How many more ladybirds than spiders were spotted? And how many fewer butterflies than ants were seen?

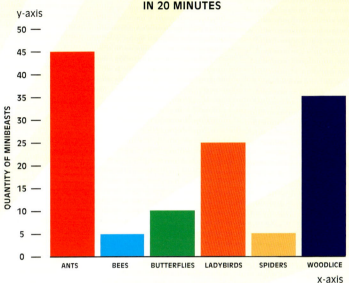

NUMBER OF MINIBEASTS SPOTTED IN THE WILDLIFE GARDEN IN 20 MINUTES

y-axis

QUANTITY OF MINIBEASTS: 50, 45, 40, 35, 30, 25, 20, 15, 10, 5, 0

ANTS · BEES · BUTTERFLIES · LADYBIRDS · SPIDERS · WOODLICE

x-axis

Scales can go up in groups of numbers (5s, 10s and 100s) so large amounts of **data** can be presented easily and clearly.

On a **graph** or **chart**, the **horizontal** line is called the **x-axis** and the **vertical** line is called the **y-axis**.

First you need to use the scale on the **y-axis** of the graph to work out how many ladybirds were spotted altogether. Notice the scale goes up in 5s.

The top of the ladybirds' bar reads 25 and the top of the spiders' bar reads 5. This means there were 25 ladybirds and 5 spiders spotted in the wildlife garden during your lesson. The sum to work out how many more ladybirds than spiders were spotted is:

$25 - 5 = 20$

You can see 45 ants and 10 butterflies were spotted in the wildlife garden and the sum to work out how many fewer butterflies than ants were spotted is:

$45 - 10 = 35$

Now try this...

How many minibeasts did you and your classmates see altogether?

 20 more ladybirds than spiders were spotted in the wildlife garden during the 20-minute lesson, and 35 fewer butterflies than ants.

15

HOW MANY BIRDS ARE IN THE TREE?

24 birds land in the tree next door. You count 53 birds altogether. How many birds were already in the tree before the others joined them?

To calculate how many birds were in the tree before more birds arrived, you must subtract the number of birds that arrived from the total number of birds. Column subtraction will keep your numbers neat and help you avoid mistakes.

T	U	
₄5	₁3	
2	4	−
	9	

Always start with the units (U) column. 3 minus 4 doesn't work; you need to take 1 from the tens (T) column and work out 13 minus 4. Write your answer at the bottom of the units column.

T	U	
₄5	₁3	
2	4	−
2	9	

Now work on the numbers in the tens column.

4 − 2 = 2

Write 2 in the answer box at the bottom of the tens column.

So 53 minus 24 is 29.

So there were 29 birds in the tree already.

You can check your answer using the **inverse operation**:

T	U	
2	9	
2	4	+
	3	
1		

Start with the units column.

9 + 4 = 13

Write 3 in the answer box at the bottom of the units column and write 1 under the answer box at the bottom of the tens column.

T	U	
2	9	
2	4	+
5	3	
1		

Now add the numbers in the tens column.

2 + 2 + 1 = 5

Write 5 in the answer box at the bottom of the tens column. The answer 53 shows your first answer – 29 – was correct.

There were 29 birds in the tree before the others arrived.

Make it easy!

Look for clues in the wording of the question to help you decide which **operation** to use, such as 'were already' and 'fly away'.

Always check

(1) under your answer box

(2) the tens and hundreds columns for numbers that have been **carried over**.

Now try this...

13 of the birds in the tree fly away.

How many birds can you see in the tree now?

APPROXIMATELY HOW MANY DAISIES ARE THERE?

Your brother says there are millions of daisies in your back garden but you think he's exaggerating. How many daisies are really there?

To find out how many daisies there are in your garden, first you have to work out the area.

area = width x length

Your garden is 4 metres long and 3 metres wide. Drawing a grid based on your measurements and counting the squares is one way to work out the area of the garden.

Another way is to use multiplication. You know 4 times 3 is 12.

4 x 3 = 12

So the garden is 12 square metres. You can write this as: 12 m²

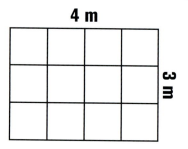

4 m

3 m

You counted 25 daisies in 1 m², so to find out approximately how many daisies are in 12 m² you need to multiply 25 by 12.

H	T	U	
	2	5	
	1	2	x
		0	
	1		

Start with the units column.

2 x 5 = 10

Put 0 in the answer box in the units column and write 1 under the answer box in the tens column.

H	T	U	
2	5		
1	2	×	
5	0		
	1		

Next, work out the sum: 2 x 2 = 4. Add the 4 and the 1 you carried over: 4 + 1 = 5. Write 5 in the answer box in the tens column.

H	T	U	
2	5		
1	2	×	
5	0		
5	0		
	1		

Write 0 in the answer box at the bottom of the units column so you don't record any of your calculations there. Work out the sum: 1 x 5 = 5. Write 5 in the answer box at the bottom of the tens column.

H	T	U	
	2	5	
	1	2	×
	5	0	
2	5	0	
	1		

Work out the sum: 1 x 2 = 2. Write 2 in the answer box in the hundreds (H) column.

H	T	U	
	2	5	
	1	2	×
	5	0	
2	5	0	
		0	

Add the numbers in the answer box. Start with the units column: 0 + 0 = 0. Write 0 under the answer box in the units column.

H	T	U	
	2	5	
	1	2	×
	5	0	
2	5	0	
3	0	0	
1			

Next, add the answer box numbers in the tens column: 5 + 5 = 10. Write 0 in the tens column and put 1 at the bottom of the hundreds column.

Then add the numbers in the hundreds column: 2 + 1 = 3. Write 3 in the answer box.

So there are approximately 300 daisies in your back garden ... not millions!

Make it easy!

Always **start** with the **units column** when you are doing column calculations.

Working something out approximately is the same as estimating. When you **estimate**, you **round** numbers **up** or **down** to the nearest **whole number**, 10 or **multiple** of 10.

Now try this...

Your neighbour's garden is 9x7 metres and there are **approximately** 6 daisies in 1 m². Does their garden have more or fewer daisies in it?

HOW MANY ANTS DOES IT TAKE TO CARRY A GRAPE?

You are watching some ants carrying twigs and leaves to their nest as you munch on some grapes in your garden. This makes you start to wonder how many ants it would take to carry a grape.

Most ants weigh 0.003 grams and can carry 100 times their own weight. A small seedless grape weighs 3 grams.

So, to work out how much weight 1 ant can carry, first you must multiply 0.003 grams by 100.

When you multiply a decimal by 100 the number moves 2 places to the left of the decimal point.

0	.	0	0	3
← ×100				
0	.	3		

0.003 x 100 = 0.3

So, 1 ant can carry 0.3 grams.

When you multiply a decimal by 10 the number moves 1 place to the left of the decimal point.

0	.	3	
← ×10			
3	.	0	

You already know 1 ant weighs 0.3 g and 1 grape weighs 3 g. If you move the 3 in 0.3 one place to the left of the decimal point, you get 3.

0.3 x 10 = 3

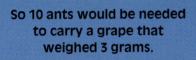

So 10 ants would be needed to carry a grape that weighed 3 grams.

Make it easy!

To **multiply** a number by **10** just write **0** at the end.

3 x 10 = 30
33 x 10 = 330
333 x 10 = 3,330

To **multiply** a number by **100** just write **00** at the end.

3 x 100 = 300
33 x 100 = 3,300
333 x 100 = 33,300

To **divide** a number by **10** remove **0** from the end or move it 1 place to the right of the **decimal point**.

300 ÷ 10 = 30
30 ÷ 10 = 3
3 ÷ 10 = 0.3

To **divide** a number by **100** remove **00** from the end or move it 2 places to the right of the **decimal point**.

300 ÷ 100 = 3
30 ÷ 100 = 0.3
3 ÷ 100 = 0.03

Now try this...

How many ants would it take to carry a cherry that **weighed 6 grams?**

HOW MANY LINES OF SYMMETRY IN A HONEYCOMB HEXAGON?

Your family keeps bees. When you collect the honey, you notice the honeycomb is hexagonal. How many lines of **symmetry** are there?

A line of symmetry has exactly the same image on either side of it. It is sometimes called a mirror line because if you put a mirror on it, the reflection would look exactly the same as the image behind it.

Some shapes have 1 line of symmetry.
This leaf shape looks the same on both sides of the line and it is only symmetrical down this line.

Other shapes, like the side view of this bee, have no lines of symmetry.

Then there are shapes that have more than 1 line of symmetry. The hexagon in this honeycomb has lots of lines of symmetry. You can draw a line of symmetry from each corner to the opposite corner and from the centre of each side to the centre of the opposite side.

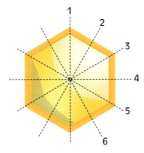

There are 6 lines of symmetry in a hexagon.

Make it easy!

An **equilateral triangle** has **3 lines of symmetry.**

A **square** has 4 lines of symmetry.

A **rectangle** has 2 lines of symmetry.

A **trapezium** has 1 line of symmetry.

You can trace a shape and then fold the paper to find if there are any **lines of symmetry.**
If 2 sides fit together exactly the shape is **symmetrical.**

Now try this...

How many lines of symmetry are there on this ladybird?

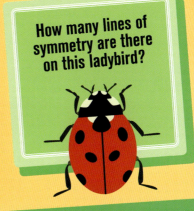

WHAT IS THE SPEED OF EACH ANIMAL?

You want to work out the speed of a cheetah, a brown hare and a gazelle. From a nature book, you have learned several facts.

Sometimes a hungry cheetah can run 2 kilometres in 1 minute.
A brown hare being chased can run 1 kilometre in 2 minutes. (It can run even faster over short distances!)
A herd of gazelle can run 4 kilometres in 3 minutes.

But what is the speed of each animal in kilometres per hour?

Because speed is usually measured in kilometres (or miles) per hour, you have to work out the distance each animal runs in one hour.

To turn the cheetah's 1-minute run into its speed, divide 60 minutes by the 1 minute it ran for:

$60 \div 1 = 60$

Then multiply your answer by 2 kilometres:

$60 \times 2 = 120$

So, a cheetah's top speed is 120 kilometres per hour.

(Cheetahs can't actually run this fast for a whole hour. They can only run this fast for a very short amount of time!)

To turn the brown hare's 2-minute run into its speed, divide 60 minutes by the 2 minutes it ran for:

$60 \div 2 = 30$

Then multiply your answer by 1 kilometre:

$30 \times 1 = 30$

So, a brown hare's top speed is 30 kilometres per hour.

To turn the gazelle's 3-minute run into its speed, divide 60 minutes by the 3 minutes it ran for:

$60 \div 3 = 20$

Then multiply your answer by 4 kilometres:

$20 \times 4 = 80$

So, a gazelle's speed is 80 kilometres per hour.

Make it easy!

Convert minutes into hours to make your calculations easier.

60 minutes = 1 hour

30 minutes = ½ hour

15 minutes = ¼ hour

Speed is the distance something can travel in a certain amount of time.

Now try this...

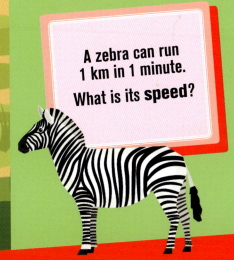

A zebra can run 1 km in 1 minute.

What is its **speed**?

A cheetah's speed is 120 kilometres per hour, a brown hare's speed is 30 kilometres per hour and a gazelle's speed is 80 kilometres per hour.

coordinates

WHICH ANIMALS WILL YOU VISIT AT THE ZOO?

Your friend has planned a zoo tour for you so you can visit all your favourite animals around the zoo. They have given you these **coordinates**:

(7, 7), (1, 2), (7, 3), (3, 2), (5, 6).

Which animals will you visit?

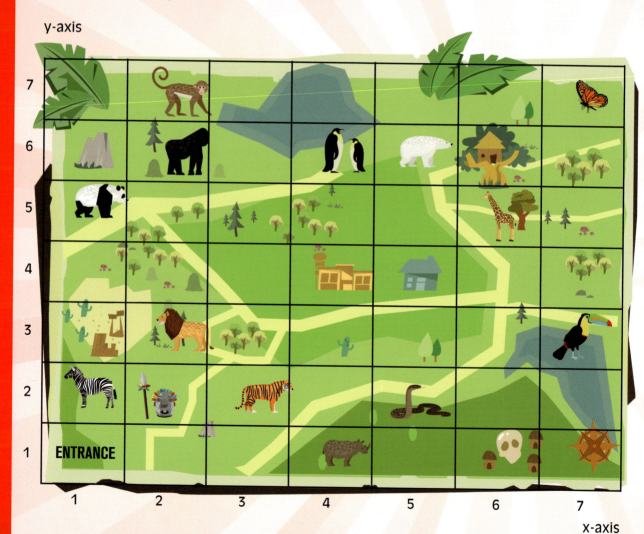

26

To find (7,7), look at the numbers on the x-axis and the y-axis. The entrance is at coordinate (1, 1) because that's the square where the numbers one and one meet on the map.

So the coordinates (7, 7) are easy to read. You just find the square where seven and seven meet.

But where is (1, 2)? If you look at the map, there are two places where the numbers one and two meet. Only one of these places has animals in it. So this must mean that when we read coordinates, we read the number on the x-axis first and then the number on the y-axis.

Now you know this, (7, 3) should be easy to find. You find seven along the horizontal x-axis and then move up three squares on the vertical y-axis.

The last two coordinates are tricky. For each coordinate, there are two possible animals to visit but only one of them is the correct one. It all depends on whether you can read the coordinates in the right order.

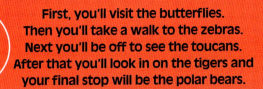

First, you'll visit the butterflies. Then you'll take a walk to the zebras. Next you'll be off to see the toucans. After that you'll look in on the tigers and your final stop will be the polar bears.

Make it easy!

An easy way to remember which order to read **coordinates**:

You go along the corridor (**x-axis**) and then up the stairs (**y-axis**).

Another way to help you remember which order to read **coordinates** is: X comes before Y in the alphabet.

Now try this...

Give your friend the **coordinates** for the snakes, the gorillas and the giraffes.

WHICH IS THE BEST BEACH FOR OBSERVING SEA TURTLES?

You have volunteered to help the sea rangers on the Hawaiian Island of Maui, who are working on a project to protect the Hawaiian green sea turtle. It is your job to look at online data and work out which beach is best for turtle spotting.

The data for Kapalua Bay is presented in a **tally** chart. It shows the amount of turtles seen at 5 different times of day.

Sunrise	|||| |||| |||| |||| |||| |||| |||| |||| ||||
Midday	|||| |||| |||| |||| |||| |||| |||| ||
Afternoon	|||| |||| |||| |||| ||||
Sunset	|||| |||| ||||	
Midnight	|||| |||

The data for Ho'okipa Beach Park is displayed in a bar chart. It also shows the amount of turtles seen at 5 different times of day.

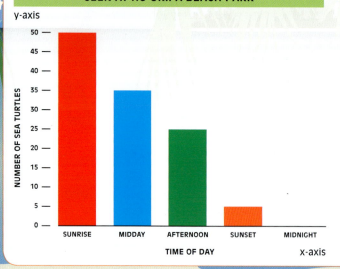

BAR CHART SHOWING NUMBER OF SEA TURTLES SEEN AT HO'OKIPA BEACH PARK

At first glance, there does not seem to be much difference between the 2 beaches. You can see from both charts that the best time of day to see the turtles is at sunrise and that there are fewer turtle sightings as the day goes on.

You need to add up the total amount of sightings on each beach to find out which beach is best for spotting turtles.

Use your 5 times table to total up the tally chart. First count all the groups of 5:

5 x 25 = 125

Then count the units. There are 6.

Add your totals together: 125 + 6 = 131.

131 turtles were sighted at Kapalua Bay.

Read the numbers at the top of each bar on your bar chart, write them in a column and then add them up.

H	T	U	
	5	0	
	3	5	
	2	5	
		5	+
1	1	5	
1	1		

115 turtles were sighted at Ho'okipa Beach Park.

So there were more turtle sightings at Kapalua Bay.

To find out exactly how many, you need to take away the number of turtles seen at Ho'okipa Beach Park from the number of turtles seen at Kapalua Bay.

H	T	U	
1	2₃	₁1	
1	1	5	−
	1	6	

Kapalua Bay is best for turtle spotting because 16 more turtles were seen there on the day of the survey.

Make it easy!

Tally charts are used to collect **data** quickly. They are easy to read as you can **count up** numbers in groups of 5.

Bar charts are good for comparing because **amounts** shown as bars are very easy to understand at a glance.

Now try this...

How many more sea turtles were spotted at sunrise compared to sunset?

GLOSSARY

> A mathematical symbol meaning greater than, e.g. 12 > 8 means 12 is greater than 8.

< A mathematical symbol meaning less than, e.g. 8 < 12 means 8 is less than 12.

Angle The measurement between 2 lines that start at the same point. Angles are measured in degrees (°). A right angle measures exactly 90°, an acute angle measures less than 90° and an obtuse angle measures more than 90°.

Axis The lines framing a graph or chart. The horizontal line is called the x-axis. The vertical line is called the y-axis.

Bar chart A chart that displays data using rectangular bars of different heights.

Coordinates Pairs of numbers that show the exact position on a map or graph. The first number shows how far along a point is on the x-axis and the second number shows how far up a point is on the y-axis.

Data Facts and numbers collected together to study something or write a report on it.

Denominator The bottom number in a fraction, e.g. the denominator of ⅖ is 5.

Equilateral triangle A triangle with 3 equal sides and 3 equal angles.

Equivalent The same as. Equivalent fractions are fractions that are the same size as each other e.g. ½ and ¼.

Estimate Round numbers up or down in sums to provide a good guess.

Horizontal A flat line from left to right.

Inverse operation The opposite operation, e.g. addition is the inverse of subtraction; multiplication is the inverse of division, doubling is the inverse of halving.

Mnemonic A word, phrase or poem that helps you remember something.

Numerator The top number in a fraction, e.g. the numerator of ⅔ is 2.

Operation The 4 mathematical operations are addition (+), subtraction (–), multiplication (x) and division (÷).

Perimeter The distance all the way around a 2D shape.

Symmetry An object has symmetry if a line going through it shows a mirror image on both sides.

Tally 4 vertical lines crossed diagonally by a fifth to represent a group of 5. Used to collect data quickly, e.g. ⦀⦀

Vertical A line that goes straight up.

NOW TRY THIS... ANSWERS

Page 5

$32 - 8 = 24$

There would be 24 wings altogether.

Page 7

$72 \times 2 = 144$

Your tallest sunflower is 144 centimetres high.

Page 9

6 and 12 can both be divided by 6.

$6 \div 6 = 1$

$12 \div 6 = 2$

So, ½ (half) of the rabbits are still outside.

Page 11

$5 \times 2 = 10$

$88 + 10 = 98$

The perimeter of the wildlife garden is now 98 metres.

Page 13

There are 4 obtuse angles altogether.

Page 15

$45 + 5 + 10 + 25 + 5 + 35 = 125$

There were 125 minibeasts spotted altogether.

Page 17

$53 - 13 = 40$

There are 40 birds left in the tree.

Page 19

$9m \times 7m = 63m^2$ $63 \times 6 = 378$

There are approximately 378 daisies in your neighbour's garden, which is more than in your garden.

Page 21

Each ant can carry 0.3 grams so 10 ants can carry 3 grams.

If 10 ants can carry 3 grams then 20 ants can carry 6 grams.

The cherry weighs 6 grams.

It would take 20 ants to carry the cherry.

Page 23

There is 1 line of symmetry in the ladybird.

Page 25

$60 \div 15 = 4$

$15 \times 4 = 60$

The zebra has a speed of 60 kilometres per hour.

Page 27

The snakes are at (5, 2).

The gorillas are at (2, 6).

The giraffes are at (6, 5).

Page 29

$50 + 45 = 95$

$16 + 5 = 21$

$95 - 21 = 74$

74 more turtles were seen at sunrise than at sunset.

First published in paperback in Great Britain in 2020 by Wayland
Copyright © Hodder and Stoughton, 2018

Produced for Wayland by Dynamo
Written by: Anita Loughrey

ISBN: 978 1 5263 0797 2

Wayland, an imprint of
Hachette Children's Group
Part of Hodder and Stoughton
Carmelite House
50 Victoria Embankment
London EC4Y 0DZ

An Hachette UK Company
www.hachette.co.uk
www.hachettechildrens.co.uk

Printed in China

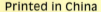

MIX
Paper from
responsible sources
FSC® C104740
FSC
www.fsc.org

10 9 8 7 6 5 4 3 2 1